Remission
(A Collection of Writing.)

FOREWARD

Behold— *my heart*. Clean and dry, pressed neatly between 140 cream colored pages.
Remission, many years ago, nameless and weightless, floated in my mind as a daydream.
My love for writing budded in childhood.
Curious and to myself most of the time, I framed, sorted and understood my experiences through writing. I wrote poetry, short stories and journaled my heart out. At that time, mostly *top secret materials*, the messy and explicit documentations of becoming. I imagined one day I would be writing books, telling my stories, and sharing my introspect— a quiet aspiration; something in a dream cloud far above my head, far in the future, if anywhere at all. I wandered in and out of love with writing, realizing I was some good at it and some bad at it, but I always came back for a good outpouring.

I struggled with the idea of sharing my writing with others, as I kept it intimate and personal for so long. I worried, what will people think when I display the imperfections and insanities I have worked so hard to conceal? For someone who works so diligently to keep quiet and in control— what will happen at this drawbridge? Eventually I barged past myself and I began to share my writing online. Over time, I grew a small audience of people who truly saw and felt themselves, hidden in the words I shared. This alone was a victory I never imagined possible, a fullness I'd never felt, and a deep hope manifested into reality. Magic before my eyes. Connection. A voice— *my voice,* being expanded with love, wielded for good. From this I had awoken an old courageous dream— publishing a book of my own.

Remission itself includes poetry and short pieces of writing over many years, some as old as my teens. There are few inclusions from that era, per most of my writing then was hysterically emotional and chaotically underdeveloped. Even now, I have some things to polish. That's the beauty of poetry, though. There's more freedom to leave it organic, raw, as messy as it is true. I have forgiven myself for those errors, grammatical and actual, and that forgiveness has something to do with the book's purpose as well.

The pieces are organized to represent a timeline of self evolution. Something I want to highlight is the necessary process of *unlearning*. There is a mindset shift happening slowly with each page turn, from approaching life and love from a place of codependency and low self worth, and then learning through the hardest moments to take after, love, and respect myself. In that, I realized what was truly necessary, and found a way to shed the burdens of my past.

Remission— the title, by all of its definitions, perfectly delineates this sometimes sightless and excruciating process of finding and forgiving oneself, healing from trauma, and declaring personal freedom from past circumstances, attachments, and self beliefs.

As for thanks and dedication, that's easy— *Remission* is a love letter, tenderly written for whomever it resonates with. This work is close to my heart and a direct representation of personal experience, but also, a shared experience, and a human experience. With love, I let go of this work and trust wherever it lands. I have tons of gratitude to express surrounding the amazing support I've had in production of this book. My beloved friends and family of course, even those who were not so kind— I have been taught by every single thing in this life, even if it came to me in hindsight. I plan to continue learning by every hand I am dealt, maybe even turning it into a poem or two. Honorary thanks to myself for keeping big promises.

Without further adieu, and so very thankful to say, I give you *Remission*.

Remission
(A Collection of Writing)

-re·mis·sion;

1. the cancellation of a debt, charge, or penalty.
2. a diminution of the seriousness or intensity of disease or pain.
3. *forgiveness of sins.*

People think change
Is an elegant task.
Like we powder our noses,
And part our hair a new way.
And suddenly we are this woman,
Who is everything we hoped to be.
As if the caterpillar
Did not curl itself tight,
Lay upside down.
Starved.
In the dark.
Before it ever emerged with wings.

As if it did not rely on—
And follow it's instincts.
Because there were no instructions.
There was no privilege
To cling to the familiar.

I tell them,
the only elegance in change—
Is in the way you fly away,
From your own corpse.

—*Metamorphosis.*

I learned
from a very young age,
-Too young to possibly be fair,
Staring into my eyes
Must be just like
staring
straight up to the sun.

God gently placed
Two twinkling umber eyes
In my frizzy little head.

I went
walking about in this world,
And found
Looks could *truly kill,*
Or- *clutch you hard
by the neck.*
And make you pay attention,
At the very least.

Lethal curiosity- I think,
made my matches for some time.
Cupid himself
drug bold, stupid men
to my doorstep.
*Well. He didn't talk to
God first, about that.*

I had to learn
Confidence speaks for itself.
Arrogance is louder.
And I have something to be *pursued.*

I mistakenly measured their *desire*
as all the more reason to try
with them;
For them.

I came to learn –
Thieves and kidnappers have great ambition too.

The trees whispered, 'oh no,'
and the squares in the sidewalk winced in suspense
under my every step
I pulled open that heavy door
and the moon turned to her stars,
wide eyed
she told her children
to close their eyes
though they tried
they only shined instead
on the top of my pretty naive head
all the flowers on the ground pulled in their bellies
and held in their breath—
I smiled and said hello to you.

"Where is this going?"
I ask you, without asking you.
I look deeper into your eyes.
Surprised I haven't crashed
Into the wall yet.
The great wall of indifference,
They all had before.

I dove deep into them,
Only to find
That down within 'em,
There is no air,
And there is no light.
Not a sound.

"So—where is this going?"
I say, without saying.
You lean in,
And I don't flinch.
Everything I am made of
Agrees with you, in my space.

I will never forget
The certain bliss of this.
Now.
I must find out—
Where this is going.

It's late
I'm stretching my fingers straight
And I'm—
tracing my name
down your back.
You know,
My first-
your last.
We're only here
Because heaven was full
For the night.
You took off your wings,
tangled yourself with me,
You smudged gold on my nose.
You put kisses all over my cheeks.

Good omen.
Little light.
Caught Fire.
Inside.

>	A sign.
>	A soothing.
>	A thrill.

Good omen.
Little light.
Soft kiss.
Big smile.

>	A longing.
>	A place
>	To call home.
>
>	Somewhere
>	I just might
>	Belong.

Good omen.
Little light.
Flickering
Inside my chest.
A sign blinking,

>	*"Come home."*
>	*"Come home."*

Let me tell you plainly.
I'm not her.
And now I have to remember,
You are not him.
This is instinctual—The safest affirmation we'll ever know.
You brush my bruises with satin fingers.
And I get the oddest knowing;
Every scar on my skin,
every hair on top of my head,
every beat of my heart sighs,
 "finally."

I promise to watch you close.
Tell your story later.
Love you through it.
And if they want to know, I will let them know—
You are my muse.
You are one half of this whole world.
The word 'forever' is tiring all on its own.
But, I will start over each day
With everything I have,
trying to give you everything you deserve.

My walls were so high
I don't even think I knew-
What was on the other side.

One thing I learned about you,
You sure can climb.

And when we return to the ashes, my love
we become one again. In the cold soil we are destined to sleep.
When their eyes have finally turned away from us.
And when all their whispers have ceased.

I have not written the ending to our story.
There never was one. There will never be.
and when we return to the ashes, my love—
I will be between the blades of grass with you.
in the deep deep roots.
underneath the plum trees.

No—I don't doubt that I knew you.
I don't doubt that I knew you, at all.
I met you before the ocean poured itself down to the basins of the earth.
I knew you before the sky filled up in beautiful blue.
We were much before
Stars burst above,
drifted up over our heads.
I knew you before there were fish in the sea.
I knew you when there was nothing.
Even then,
your scent was in my nose.
Even then,
your taste was on my tongue.

I heard them say,
The middle is just right.
That is the center of all whole things.
Often associated with
Equality and balance.
All the things we aspire for.
So, the middle is just right.
Except. When—
It's the *hardest* part.
The *confusing* part.
The *nameless* part.
And deep in my soul I know,
lukewarm
Is much more unsettling
Then the cold.

I don't want perfect.
How does perfect grow?
How does it breathe?
How does perfect learn?

I have bitten my tongue for so long
I am surprised
It will still give me words when I open my mouth.
I know, maybe more than most,
How burdensome it is
To let the bad guy get away with it.
Perhaps I have this irrational notion
My good deeds are up on a drawing board somewhere
And for all the times I imploded rather than exploded,
Took my frustrations out on myself,
Asked permission for all the things that already belonged to me,
And I kept my mouth closed
When they deserved the *bite*—

Is there a warm place waiting for the merciful?
Is there a heaven for the kind?

Why is that women
Crave more than anything else
The perceived comfort
Of big heavy arms
gripping us tight.
Have we forgotten?
At our most weak,
At our first mouthful of air,
We were held gently
In the soft arms of a woman.

Not of theirs.
But of our own.

And when you pray for him,
For the first time,
Then you may as well also
confess to God—
You are in love.

—Now, she knows.

You know,
I've been down and out
And I've had times that were
Darker than any black
I knew could be.
I've been shattered and battered.
And I've been my own sworn enemy.
You rolled up your sleeves
Reached into that bottomless pool
To come save me.
And I will always find reasons to love you.
Even on these days
When I hear from you less and less.
And I love you dearly and certainly.
Because you loved my mess.

"—If I fall asleep thinking of you, does that keep you safe?"

Slow and steady. Yes.
Slow and steady can win
The race.
But, what I'd give.
To push off the ground,
With our every fiber.
To absolutely burst toward
That line.
A feeling that comes
From acceleration.
From exhilaration.
When I think of you,
I just catch fire.
I could win the sprint.
But oh, *how I want you.*
Dedicated.
in full capacity.
Consistently.
Like a marathon.

—*Blood racing.*

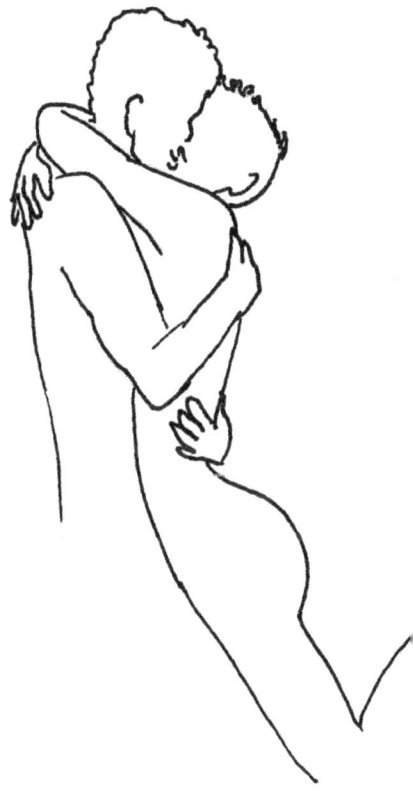

*I am convinced that your face is painted
On the inside of my eyelids.
I know, your name must've been carved
On the ceiling of my skull.*

Maybe when I was kissing you,
I took in fragments of you,
And they're busy rushing through my blood
making me sweat,
making me awfully sad,
and numbing me, too.

*When I was young,
yours,
and as open as the sky—*
I remember the euphoria that came
With the smallest touches you gave.

I had
Big bright brown eyes
And a chest much too small for my swollen soul.
Your love kept me so warm
For such a long time.
Since then, the summers are never warm enough.

You bit off more than you could chew with me.
This is usually the case.
I know better than to cry about it.
You knew I was pleasing to look at.
Didn't think I would be so hard to swallow.
Sugar on the tongue.
Fire in your throat.
yanking red roses from their beds
hungry to possess them instead.
But the flesh of your palms is too thin
To clutch the wild stem.

Now you will bleed.
For thieving.

—You salivate for kryptonite.

I can't understand why
You want to cover yourself in daisies
And speak with a bow of lies around your tongue.
Paint crusted around your face,
Making eyes at me.
But, I see what is underneath.
You want to hold my hand loosely.
Spin me dizzy in circles.
Spoil me in melodramatic mediocrities.

Does this paltry act
Of stringing me along
Help you pull
Your own
identity together

?

If the answer is no,
Like a thud in your gut.
Like a shiver in your spine.
Like a boulder on your chest.

If the answer is no,
Like the heat underneath heavy eyes.
Like the ringing of lonesome ears.
Like the aching of the tired mind.

If the answer is no,
Like waiting for nothing.
Like the wordless goodbye.

If the answer is no,
Say, okay.

You had better correct yourself.
When you see a woman's knees.
Collar bones.
Ankles.
Sides.

And you think she is saying,
Anything-
To you or for you.
To anyone for that matter.

Anything—
she has not opened her mouth,
and said for herself.

— Who will stop your eyes from gossiping to your mind?

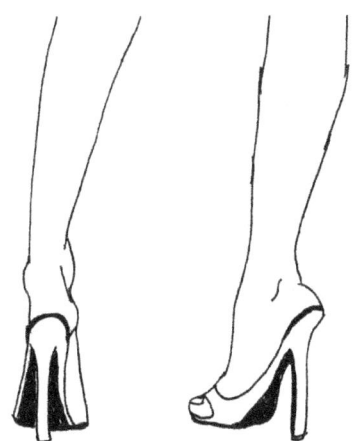

One small thing,
I both fear and know.
You cannot fill this void.

What's worse than you leaving me
And hurting me—
Is if you stay,
And you love me.

And still
I had this hole.

As I age.
I realize.
Adults are just children.
In bigger shells.

And the world is an ugly place.
If you let it.
A mistake only sticks to you
If you don't love yourself enough
To bathe it away.
Wash off a day.
A night.
A year, or two.

Time is not on my side.
So I am a woman.
Who allows herself
To grow old.

Wearing my love.
In confidence.
In comfort.
In contentment.

I know, I'm not all better.
I know sometimes I still
Want the wrong kind of things.

I know that everything in me
Wanted you.

I took all the red flags you gave me.
Unwound the thread of my hopes.
And I sewn a blanket.
To keep us warm.
And to keep the doubts out.

But I was always under that cover alone.
And you were always the monster on the other side.

All that running from my past—
I crashed straight into you.

The life we made,
was supposed to be *never ending.*
We were supposed to end up
At an alter somewhere
Kissing eagerly, surrounded by our own light.

We were supposed to grow older than this,
I was supposed to still have you at 25.

But the honey fell from our lips and we grew plain.
As I relentlessly *chose you,* over and over again.
Forgiving you, each gloomy morning.
But you chose to fade.

When you turned your back in this bed
You started to mean it.
I couldn't be forgiven for my mistakes.

—25

When did you decide I wasn' the one for you?
One day you woke up and turned over to see me
sleeping soundly
and you thought to yourself,
not of how the sun kissed my face—
But of how much space I was taking up beside you.

While you are healing,
And the weight of it
Makes you lean.
You may be between
Rocks and hard places,
Crutches and cushions,
Pillows stitched with familiarity.
Redemption linen— feels like silk
Brushing against tired skin.
Do not lean into toxicity,
Not even for a second.
Spikes lie beneath the feathers.
You know it, too.

You rouse with the past, dear-
You get pierced by its pain, too.

—It is not better than nothing.

There is an ease.
There is a reaction.
There is a behavior.
Involved with
Being in love.

*It makes you colorful.
You cannot hide it.*

So when
You cannot quite tell
If he loves you;

Remember,
If you cannot *see it*
taste it,
feel the spectrum of it
Radiating
Down of the base of your spine—

Then your answer
is just
black and white.

—*Colors.*

I could've sworn the moment I met you,
I started to *bruise*.

I just hold back so much. I resent that. I want most to be a candid human being. To let my shoulders fall. To ramble about the things that I love. To lazily find my way to the end of a sentence- just a piece at a time.

It's an excruciating pain to be misunderstood. I wonder if anyone could ever be patient enough to decode my chaotic mental and emotional habits. Help me be close and loving. Calm and liberated. *Too often I am distant and unwound. A melancholy sea of listlessness.* And I am not an advocate for this behavior. I wish I were more flowing and precise.

I wish I didn't think of myself as love charity. As a burden. As a girl who doesn't know where to start, and once she starts, she doesn't know where to finish. To talk like rain. To ache like thunder. I wish I wouldn't see myself in this way—a handful of hot coal. Only to be held for so long until I become simply unbearable.

Every time my hair grows out of my head
Someone twines their dirty fingers through it
And it stretches across pillowcases
Stained with clouded intentions
And my sheer ignorance.

I have to cut it off.

There are times when I'm okay with it.
This undeniable, boldly etched
Fact of the matter.

When I was made.
Up in space.
*When God's soft hands
Kneaded my soul.*
There was a divergence.

Instead of starting over.
I was thrust down.
Not angrily—
with aplomb.

*Hurled. Expelled. Shot to.
The earth.*
Despite the extra depths.
extra grooves and glitches.
Extra lifetimes—
I owned.

*Something I always knew how to do;
Tell my stories.
They are my flesh.
They are my compositions.*
Just like the muscles that bind to my bones.

*Sometimes, you just know
What you are meant to do.*

—*Birth of a poet.*

A woman's heart is like her body,
Both desired and shamed.
And when she wears it bare,
She is prey.

The worst of it all,
Is these men do not deserve
To live forever.
Not even if it's pressed
Between the pages of this spiral.

Not even if it's just
In the wreckage of my head.
But, because they were unfortunate enough to find me,
Because I was unfortunate enough to be theirs.

I give them immortality.
Through my words.
Through my breath.

I exhale, I shout, scribble and scratch—
Of all the times
Love pulled me
By the hair.

When the subtle wind in your heart
Shakes your trees.

When it tells you
To Go.
When it tells you
To Stay.
When it tells you
To Wait.

You loosen the veins
In your limbs.

And you allow
Yourself to be carried.

By that strange unbroken breath
Of God in you.

—*Intuition, Was the first atlas.*

The uncensored mind mumbles
Your name
Like a beat to a song
Like a sheet over my mind.

I want you again.
I want you again.

But it's not quite that easy,
And it'd never be quite the same.
Before we know it,
We will be bickering,
Pointing our fingers,
Shouting in different languages again.

Sometimes, I think,
Oh, what the hell.
If every now and then I have to fall asleep
With the world
between us.

At least I am falling asleep
With my world
beside me.

I absolve you.
I give you forgiveness I cannot afford.
I give you
my best.

Just make it right to me.
I just want—

Just once.
Make it right to me too.

—*An Empath's Prayer*

I flattered you
You were polluted weather that came
After boredom mixed
With the insecurities,
And the ego cried her plea.

Your flattery was the *cheapest*
Bandage I could afford.
For the *deepest wound*
I'd ever had.

Dear diary,

Tonight, your pages catch my grief.
It is pouring from my eyes.

There is anger,
salivating in my mouth.

I feel fire,
Smoldering underneath my scalp.

Dear diary,
I don't have the words tonight.

But oh—
my heart.
is whaling.

When you turn up—
After you lose your balance
Up on that pedestal.

After you realize-
She is a wading pool.
And I am the Pacific.

After you spend enough nights
Falling asleep
To my white noise
Whirring in the back of your head.

When you turn up-
With your excuse in one hand,
And your amends in the other.

My tired hands will only
Be holding this grudge.

What will I be known for when I spill out onto the floor?
I'll never come back from that. I never came back from any time before. I'm here just trying to be as perfect of a flower on this wall, but we all know my print is different. We all know this is a crowded, lonesome place and I'm supposed to be balanced and brave while I have glimmers of salvation swaying in and out of my life—not knowing which ones to clutch and they move too fast as it is.

And the world has kept spinning anyway, even when I wanted it to hold on, even when I asked nicely. I wish we didn't overlook each other in this way; My silence is not a state of rest, it is not a pause of motion, *it is not a mellow in between—* I've never been to a place more thundering and noisy than my own head.

What if you learned you don't know me at all? *And I can't even decide if I want you to?*

Patience.
I've been good with
Patience.

I'm trying to understand
Where we stop
Being so patient.

Waiting on—
certain things that will

Never bloom.
Never peak.
Never satisfy.

I'm still learning
Where to draw that line.
But you—
You are teaching me.

—Half passed nine.

I spilled my coffee inside of my purse.
I'm running late to work.
I say to myself,
"You don't deserve nice things."

They told me, I am beautiful.
They told me, I am excellent.
I say to myself,
"That's not true."

An idea comes.
Opportunity knocks.
I pretend I am not home.

A favor is returned.
A gift is given.

Still, I say-
"You shouldn't have."

We will not be friends.
You don't get to discard me
And devalue me
Make me lie awake for days.

And after all of it.
*Proclaim yourself
Any friend of mine.*

Even a friend
Would not
*Be so cruel
To my heart.*

And if your
lingering is a bridge,
Sure. I will
come to it again.

*With a fist full
of matches.*

Behind this wall
You will find me
Trying to repair
The machinery of my heart.
All the screws you stripped.
All the wires you cut.

Behind this wall.
I'm working under my last light bulb.
Trying to put myself
Together again.

I know, everything is going to plan.
Not our own plans,
God knows,
that is not the case.

But a plan we cannot predict.
A plan we cannot simplify.
We cannot skip
or change.

Sometimes you know why things happen.
And sometimes you don't.
So, if you ever find out why
we couldn't have each other,
Please let me know.

—*It's not fair.*

Pay attention to me.
I speak when I don't speak.
There are confessions on my fingertips.
Humming with my eyes.

And when I finally turn my back.
I am blaring loud.

You deserve someone
Just like you.
And how you treat others.
And how you see the world.
And the standards you hold.
Thinking they are somewhere above it all.

I hope you get someone
Just like you.
as superficial and benighted,
fickle and fleeting,
limp in the spine,
As you.

And then.
I hope
You measure up.

I keep thinking how
I need to change my tone.
I'm not showing
How bright I truly am.
When I am dwindling in the
Words of the past
And people
Who have cost me peace.

Truthfully,
I smile wide most days.
Not because I want to,
But because
I want others to.

Who taught you how to love?
Was it your father,
Did he show you?
Was it the television,
Did it show you?

Did anyone
Teach you how to hold a woman
Longer than the commercial break,
And make promises to be kept
When the mood has long passed?

Who taught you
How
To stay, when it's arduous
And not like the movies?

And when those nasty flaws arise
The kind real humans bare.
In our fragile flesh and blood—

Who taught you about
Unconditional and thoughtful?

And forgiveness.
And forgiveness.
And forgiveness.

Who taught you to love?

Please ask yourself.

—Before you try to love someone, with blades in your palms.

Your voice is not needed here.
Not in this narrow space.
Not in the middle of us.
Your words will do nothing here.

This language is more thorough.
This language has no way-
to structure a lie.

It is the way you speak to me here,
That I will understand.

—*Energy*

We were going to fall in love.
A deep.
I know you knew.

Maybe it wasn't what you said,
But what the universe said.
When she stretched her arm out,
Across my pounding chest.

She said, *"you will wait."*
For sincerity. For aptitude. For capability.
"You will wait."
For understanding. For substance. For respect.

And I was so angry that she sent her message through you.
And you said it.
And I scorched throughout.
And I was so angry with you.

And now.
With my sunken chest.
With my faithfulness to fate.
Like I always am;
I am grateful for her.

—*But, I was already in love.*

There is a war
roaring
Inside of my chest.
And I am growing
weak and wounded—
Involuntarily wishing,
fighting, hoping and
Sinking my tired claws into
Memories
Steadily slipping away
From me.
And I'm
Waiting to collapse,
Waiting to surrender,
To actuality
And this aching absence
Of you
And all the *new light* and
quenching hope
You had come along with.

If you are going to *choose me*
and *love me*
and *clamp your hand on top of mine,*

You had better love me
vigorously, amorously, completely, truly—
you had better *lift me up*
and *lift me high*
and *lift me always.*

You had better keep me in the corner behind you
and *never in the one you are plowing into.*
You had better say the things that you mean
and *do the things that you say.*

And when you come through this door
after a long unkind day,
I want you to choose to love me instead.

God will make me born again.
God will make me whole.

God will open my chest right up,
And scoop this mush into a bowl.

God will laugh a hearty laugh,
And she will say to me;

"Silly girl, head of curls,
We got him out, you're free."

Come to this conclusion;
You are meant
For better things.

And life will take you to them.
Ungraciously.
Mercilessly.
Brutally.

And you will arrive at them
Bare
And
Wise.

Ready to be taken in.
Enveloped entirely.
Clothed in love.
Rewarded. beyond measure.

—Traveling

Suffering does not come by the drop.
No. Pain
Comes by the bucket.
By the boatload.

Something about
loving you—

It was like
Drinking
From a fire hose.

Remember when we
would imagine growing old
With one another.

We would.
Name children we hadn't had yet.
And.
We would write one another love letters,
ten miles long. Pictures and songs.

At that time
l*ove equaled obsession.*
Do you remember how
We kept each other awake for days?

We never had those children.
But.
Tonight, you keep me awake.

And you'll never forget;
You learned this from me.
If you wave a blossom around too fast.
It falls apart.

And if you shove it into your pockets,
You'll crush it to pieces.

And if you promise it water,
And you have none,
You will let it die.

You are not gentle nor grateful.
You should keep your hands off valuable things.

—The next time you see petals on the ground.

I'm still teaching myself
To catch that moment, midair.
When I start to slip backwards.
When I am about to crack my skull.
From the fall
or the thoughts.
Either way.
I am never fast enough.

—*Unlearning*

That strange pleasure
Of missing you.
Preserving you.
In my head.

That strange pain-
Of missing you.
Pretending with you.
Knowing that is all it'll ever be.

—*Loop.*

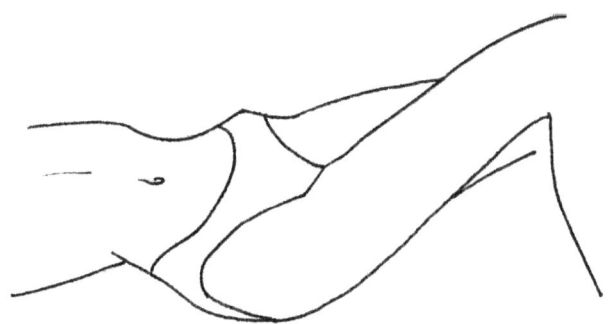

There's something to be said about the stories never written down. There is something to be said about memories you choose not to savor, but rather wish you could spit out, or bury entirely.

Whatever you write, lives. I tried to keep you alive long beyond your expiration. I cupped you in my palms, *wilted and rotten—* I ran my fingers through the soil where you slept until I *could not feel my hands.* I knew you weren't returning to me; you were not underwater, lovesick, or beside yourself. I knew my words would only humiliate me in the end, but I still wrote. *I could not stop.*

I had days on end, somehow both *full and empty* of you. I dreamt of your mouth on my neck, *your hands full of me.* I dreamt of your insincerities, your *indifferences.* I dreamt I pointed a gun *right between your eyes.* I felt everything for you— *grief, lust, fury,* but mostly a *wanting.* A wanting that *would not sleep.* So restless, so hairy and so thorned. A wanting with serrated teeth and a warm belly for me to soak my tears into.

How have I not burst into flames yet?
How have I not ran like a waterfall, right out of this bed?

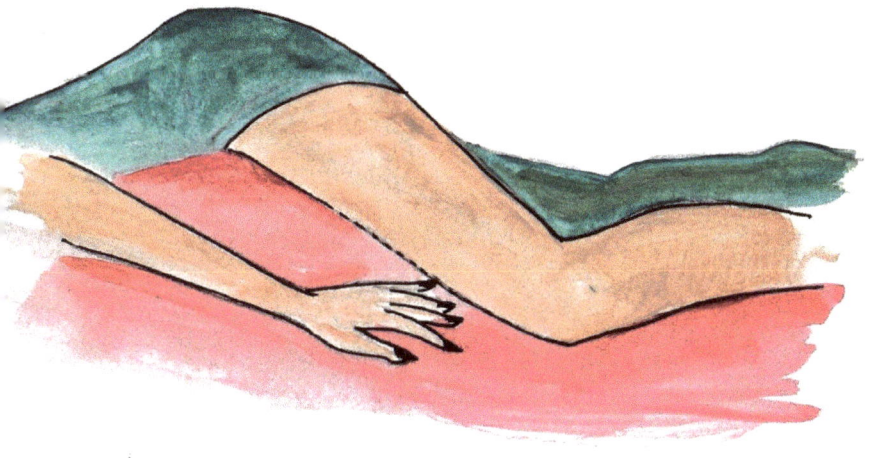

Sometimes, it is all for *nothing*.
Sometimes, you can only
look around and scream.

Too much blood.
Too much loss.

You grab a rag.
You clean it up.
You call it experience.

And you make a mildly
better mess next time.

I am no longer concerned about
Who stays and who goes.
Who loves me or who loathes me.
Whatever shuffle they are between.

Because I am the first page and the last page.
I am the hero, and I am the saved.
I make my endings, and I make my chapters.
I make my lessons.
And I print only in love;
To me, from me, about me.

Treat me with kindness.
I may lend you a few words.

I am learning
How to love you.
From all the way over here.
And it's not that I want to,
But I have to.
Because *my love*
Is *endless*.
It is more powerful
Then any resentment.

Time has taught me,
There is a special energy.
That is never destroyed.

For better or worse,
I don't swim against this current anymore.
I just hope—when a warm wind
Kisses your cheek.

You know, I am hoping
You're doing okay.

—*What forever means.*

As inconsiderate as time can be,
It has a way of licking its own wounds.

—Don't trust me. Trust tomorrow.

Everything that's needed to be said, has been said already. I often think of the dull ache in my heart and how it's not new at all. These words? hardly. Maybe for this lifetime, and maybe for this body, these hands. These eyes, mouth and tongue. But I have been here before. Felt this before. *In the pit of my heart, there is an older one.* I began in this world as the ocean floor. And you must have had a past life, too. *And you were the color blue. You must have been the rain.*

I am love.
I am love scrubbed clean; I am love fresh from the rinse.
I am love—lying out, drying out. In the sun.
I am love—beet red, pounding, present.
I am love glimmering overhead.

I am love;
And love only.
Love entirely.

I give myself permission
To accept this change. To allow this change.
To observe this change. To be this change.
To embrace this change.

To step away from what I have known.
To step into what I know now.
To shed the skin and the weight upon me.

To begin again.

There is no picture that I'll live in
that I will not paint myself.
Down to the last stroke.

It is certain—
it must please my soul.

My alone
Curls my toes.
Drenches my soul.

My alone says,
"come as you are.
I promise—
I love you, anyway."

What will set someone apart from the rest, Is when you catch a glimpse of *yourself—*Right there, within them. Like they've got a *piece of you* clutched close. Something that feels like gravity. Maybe something you never showed, never shared—never even whispered about. Just a small, intimate piece.

That's what you had. A piece of me. A secret about me. *My mother's kiss on my forehead.* You saw and spoke to the *human in me.* The *helpless* in me. Where I'd been hidden, all this time, bare and weak.

I lie my head down in your lap to be loved in this way. To be safe. To be known. You were something strange. *How you met me exactly where I stood in the world.* Came to me like a dream lingering on my eyes from every night before. Reunited. Remembered. Divine, delicate parallel. Joy born *anew*. Joys we *thought we had lost—Sewing from the same thread*. You left me feeling speechless. Complete. Content. *Sleeping like a child. In your love.*

That's what you had. Illusion of safety; *The ingredients of love-* Whatever the hell that is. Clearly, I still don't know. *I am still quietly mourning that catch and release.* tending to the residual aches. *Coming back to the burial ground with wild flowers in my hands.* Longing. Endlessly craving. A supernatural feeling I only got to taste; *never keep. My appetite still roars for that*.

I'd be better off if I still thought there couldn't be such a thing.

—*I'll never tell you. I'll never ever tell you.*

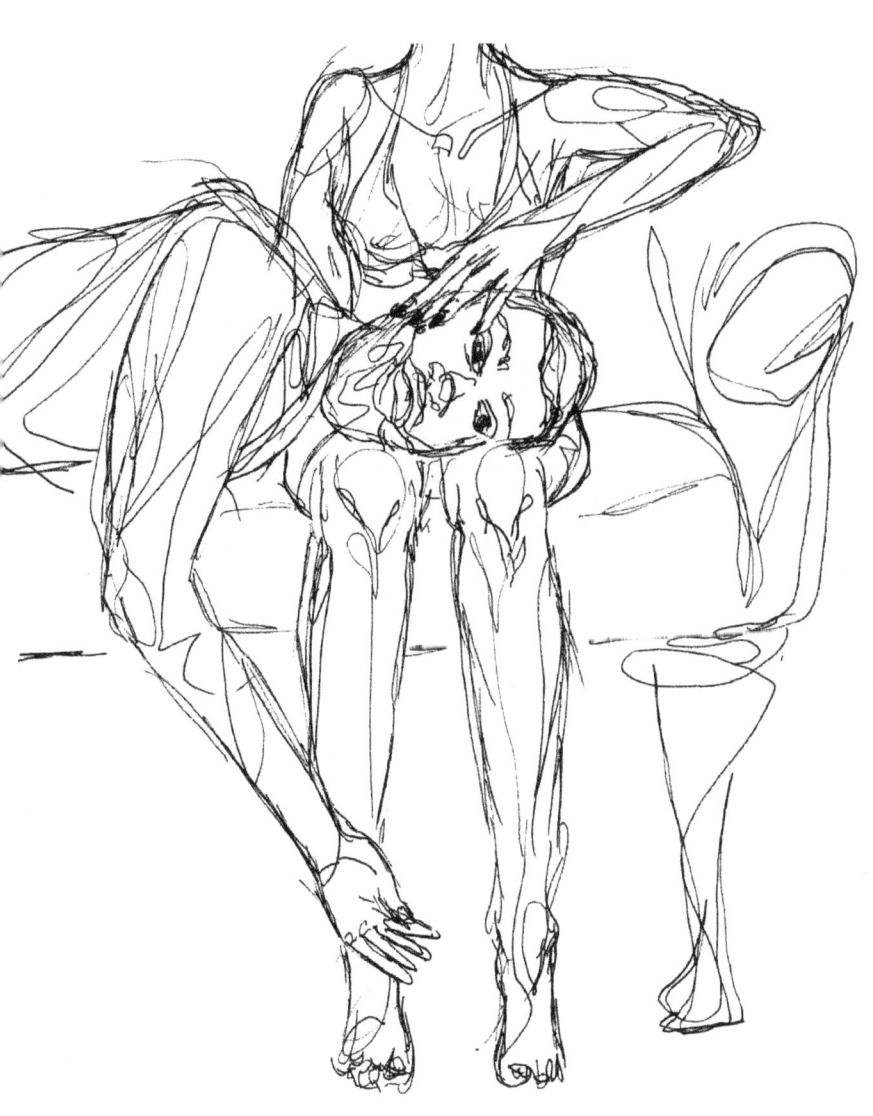

Thoughts of you
Wrap around me like twine.
Lift me up and away from myself.
They pull me across stormy skies.

I look down at her,
Living empty.
Her head, in the clouds.

—*Asleep.*

But I've done enough of that; That angry emotion just doesn't resonate with me anymore. It's growing tasteless with time. *Not sure if I've finally come over the mountain or if I have become it.*

Your power.
Call for its presence.
Call for its attendance.
Call for its commitment.
Every single day.

This morning, you—
let down another peel, you
spin out another petal, you
take another drink
from the sky.
This morning, you
claim to be worth every inch
you occupy.
This morning, you
love the cold downpour like
you love the high sun.
This morning, you
realize, they—
only together,
broke you from the seed.
raised you from the soil.

—This morning / Good Morning.

Strip me bare.
Rinse me clean.
The light in me.
Needs not—
What I have coated myself in.
And have been surrounded by.
And hid behind.

I need not.
I want not.

Strip be bare.
Rinse me clean.
The light
In me
Needs nothing.

—I don't want the weight anymore.

I don't always pray.
Sometimes my mind is away.
I worry more about what I can get my hands on.
And what I can justify.
And what can be guaranteed.

I don't always pray.
And when I do,
I feel it's wrong to come around only with a favor to ask.

I have heard so many names for you.
I wish I knew which one you like to answer to.
We're all down here, looking for your advice.
And some of us even think we know how you want things done.

I don't always pray.
But whenever I do. I fear you;
And I thank you. For every single thing.

For everything that was not love, illuminated what is.
Everything that was not good, taught me what is.
You are.

I don't always pray.
But when I do. sometimes I find tears.

One thing you make sure I know.
Is that quietly, relentlessly and without condition-
You keep with me.
Even when I think
You ought to be too disappointed in me.

I don't always pray.
But when I do.
I feel.
Your softness on the other side of the conversation.
The love in your listening.

I don't care what they say.
You are the best listener.
Because you say nothing at all.

I let you get me down
For way too long.
I never wanted to meet your ghost.
I never wanted my mind to itch all night.
Tossing around.
Drunk about you.

I want to forget.
This feeling.
Rambunctious love.
There is nowhere for it to go.

Each night, my chest grows until it breaks open.
Boiled over and empty at sunrise *and still*.
And still.
And Still— I love you.

I know that's you.
Calling out to my heart.
Feeling you on the back on my neck.
Hearing you in the quiet.
Seeing you in the dark.

Adults do not heal any faster or better.
We just swallow the lumps in our throats
Before they jump through our eyes.

Eventually they learn to live
In the pits of our guts
And behind every closed door we can find.

I stand shakily in the porcelain tub, like an infant first on its feet. Swaying my body underneath a downpour so searing that it bites at my skin—Exactly as I had ordered; *incineration*. I have parts to kill. Suds on my neck, breasts, and sides cleanse me of your touch. I watch your fingerprints rise right off of my skin, curling up around the edges, arching their backs and moaning in agony, sliding down my ankles, and drowning toward the drain. Your scent is being swallowed alive in the steam. Your shadowed image is smoldering away in the fog of it; and I know I will never look you in your eyes again. Silent prayers murmur off of my lips, the taste of you fading with every *"amen."* Pruned hands rake through my hair and I realize it has grown too long again. I finally step out—glistening, naked and empty, and *I start my life over at the sink*. I pinch my hair between two fingers and cut off whatever reaches beyond. I slather oil on my body, creams in my hair, and I air dry as not to taint my birthing ceremony. Once the color returns to my eyes, I lay on my bed until the sun burns out.

I have been softened.
Maybe for how many times I've tried
To walk through open doors
Only to find—the soles of my feet
On crushed glass and
Broken ideas.

Maybe for every time I collapsed to the ground,
Left for dead.
And I found love—right there
In between the floorboards.

Maybe for every time I locked myself in closets
And I found myself talking to the monsters that hid in them as well.
Some of them even found the courage to go on their way
Once we came to our understandings.

Maybe for every sunken chest
And drenching of cold sweat
Wrung the poison out of me like an old rag.

I've tried to bury myself in the gravel.
Become hard and impenetrable like the rocks I lie between.
And somehow, at each sunrise-
I awake.

And I am the soft yellow flowers that
Relentlessly,
gently,
Faithfully—reach above.

— *I have been softened.*

I used to think,
Oh, how lucky he would have been to have me.
I loved him so much.
I loved him over the moon.

He could have it all. with me.
In me. From me.
I suppose he'd have everything;
Except me.
Only the shell of me.

—I'm so glad you didn't stay.
 It had to be this way.
 I had to find my way.

Moments are passing
And those around me
Barely touch them with their heels.
Just push off them, tips of their toes.
They are so eager to be onto what is next.
Maybe they just don't like their feet wet.
Maybe they only want to be seen
making their glide.

Moments are passing
And I like to dig into them
Up to my waist.
I like to dip my head under
And let it drip from my nose.

Moments are passing
And I rest easy
Whether the water is hot
Or the waves come cold.

I let my fingertips prune
Touching, grasping, caressing
All over the life
That belongs to me.

What's mine is certainly coming.
And it knows where to find me.

—*Right here. / Right now*

You do not threaten my spirit anymore.
We do not crave your redemptions, anymore.
We can peel away from
The rigid layers of that time.
Your reference is but another life.

And I smile for us.
But now,
 I have elsewhere to be.

We ask a lot of love.
When are you coming?
And how deep are you?
And how good are you?
And how long will you stay?

But what do we offer it in return?
What is due
To love?
To make it *deep*.
And make it *good*.
And let it stay?

Love requires just as we do.
The space to occupy.
The breath to translate.
The body to demonstrate.
The ego to humble.

And truly— we owe love
Our whole vessel.
This entire time.
Our deepest trust.

Love is the most valuable thing
we will ever know.
And yet,
It will always be too expensive for the vain.

It takes time
To reach the goldmine.
It might be
The hardest thing you ever do.

But when you are worn
Remember you've sworn
Yourself—this to be true.

The universe molds
The light your heart holds
So just—
Stay to see it through.

Good and gracious,
And forgiving and patient.
And true.
And true.

Watching over me
Parting my path.

Trusting me to
learn.

Trusting me to
endure.

Trusting me
to succeed.

And—
I will.
I will.
I will.

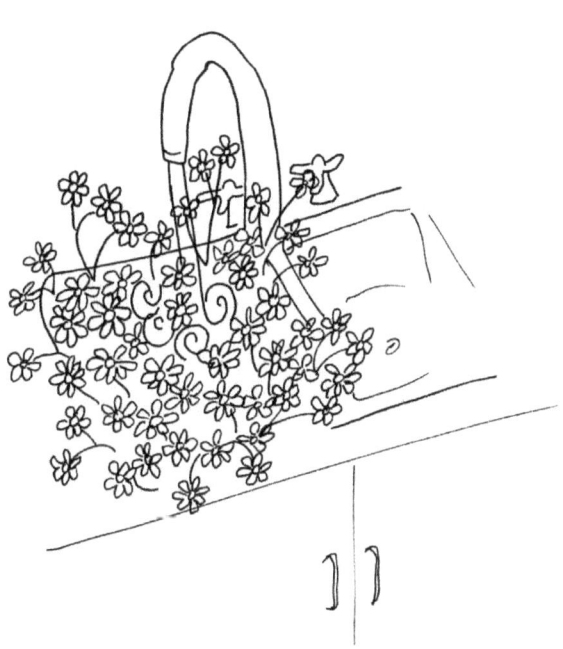

Be open, but without a web.
Be open like the air.
Let things through.
And let things go.

May you rely on this tender thought;
You are infinite.
And this body—plush and warm,
Is only one stage of your being.
Never take something here or there too harshly,
Your spirit still has many journeys to go.
Your spirit lives deeply beyond—
Unkind words and inconvenient ailments.

There are no such wounds here,
No such worries here,
That could ever keep you
from the great progression.

I am
brown skin
pointed nose
dark eyed
small boned
a violent collision of two worlds
arm wrestled into defiant curls
and crooked teeth.
I am the fruit of forbidden things;
Countless old, uncommon souls
and wild flowers that were called weeds.
I am
songs sung long after sundown
And deep red love that demanded no glory
That went seeping, bleeding
passing between wet eyes and tired hands.

I am their
Fierce fights. Quiet kisses. Whispered dreams.
I carry secrets much older than me.
I was made to know the beauty in radical things.
And, I have come a long way on these boney feet.
And I have come a long way short on sleep.
I weathered ten thousand storms before I was born
and,
I know nothing of ordinary, obedient, or permissible things.

—sometimes, I must
 gently remind myself,
 I was not made.
 to please.

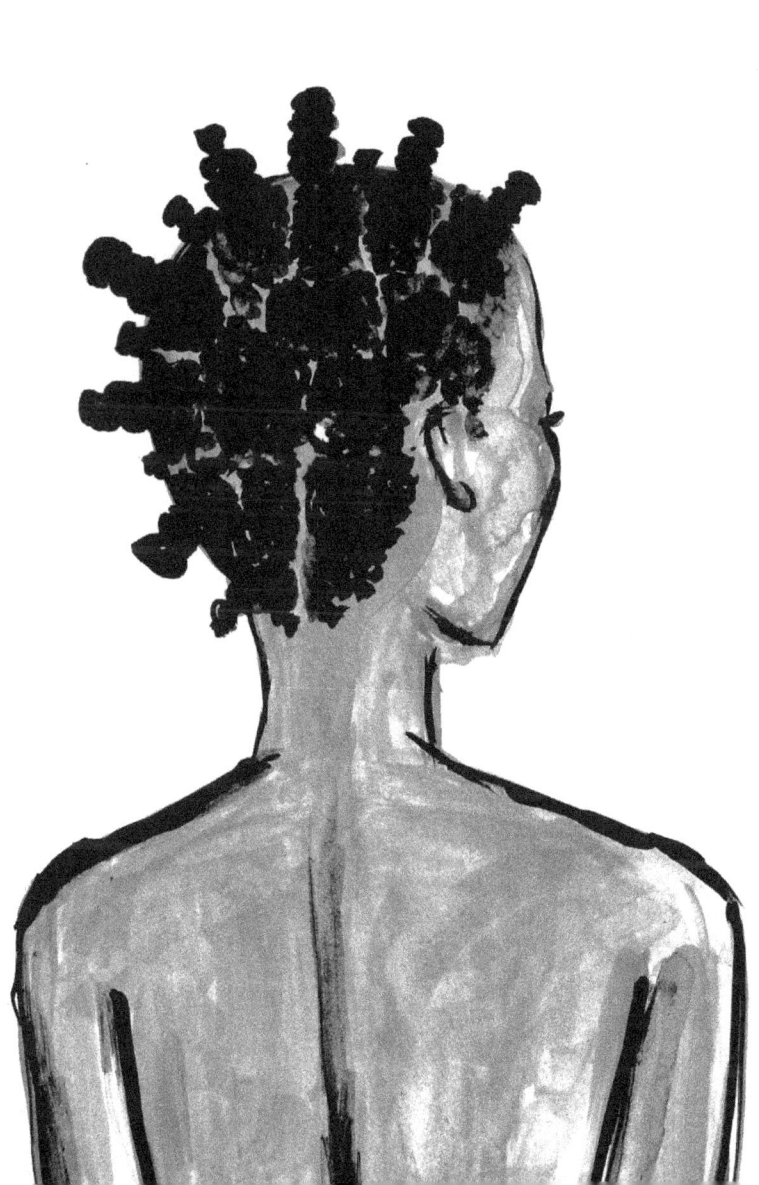

"smile."
"Keep your hands visible."
"Don't become angry."
"Don't be loud."
"Be still."
"Yes sir."
"Yes ma'am."
"Please."
"Thank you."
"I'm sorry."
"I'm sorry."
"I'm sorry."

They may teach their children.
We must train ours.

—*Call me when you get home.*

Look what you've done.
Your fears made us afraid of ourselves.

Chamomile tea before I go to sleep.
Long showers late at night.
Open the windows for fresh air.
Someday I know- I'll run into you again.
Underneath the blankets on the weekend.
Really wonder why- sometimes.
Even in my sleep- *I'm chasing after you.*

c

l

o

s

u

r

e

When I am gone
Do not hush others
When my name comes about.
I was anything but confined.

Make sure you let me live
Forever
As I was meant to.

And if my spirit lingers.
Let it have a dance in your mind.
If I ever made you smile.
Do, please—smile once more.

Darling, listen close
It is not tragic.
That I have finally
Found my way
To the odd and delicate place
I know I am from.

—Love is never meant to be buried.

What's the harm?
I dream of myself in your arms,
I long for chest achingly sweet moments
Between only us two.

You make me
Rosy cheeked and warm all over.
They say when your ears burn,
they're thinking of you, too.

—*Lullabies*

Despite my desire to be this small quant thing,
the universe continues to lovingly nag on me—
no I am anything but. I will be anything but.
Old thoughts and decisions felt like bumping my
head on the ceiling. Curling my toes up inside of my shoe.
I don't fit here anymore.
I had to take everything off.
Put everything down.
Wash everything away.
This ritual was terrifying until it was therapeutic.

I will live happily ever after.
Perhaps without much diamonds or jewels.
Perhaps without much gold and gadgets.
Still—*I will be so well.*

I will grow fruit in my garden.
Fruit in my womb.
Fruit in my heart.

—*A Juicy life.*

You know,
you are your bravest, just like this.
Learning the hard things, open hearted.
Giving up love like it'll never run out.
A monument—you are.
Courageous. Imperfect. Mighty.
God counted your head with the angels tonight.
She smiled down on you—
Moonlight.

And
this very quiet part
needs documenting
the most.
Because it is
my budding after a very long drought.
It is my mind
becoming fluid
After your coldness
and your ice
has thawed from it.
This very quiet wind—
is my migration.
this very humble light—
is my beam.

—*Liberation of heart.*

I heard the birds chatting this morning.
Talkin' about the way I fix my tea.
The way I brush my hair.
I heard the birds singing this morning.
Singin' about the way I mend myself.
The way I carry my heart.
And, it was good things for once;
maybe my ear is finally attuned.
They sang of my glory days.
"Saw them comin' over the horizon," they said.
They sang my name, and it sounded new.
They didn't care who heard.
Neither did I.

I learn myself through you.

—Thank you

QR code: www.KatrishaRose.com

Follow website link to follow current social sites and online store.

www.ingramcontent.com/pod-product-compliance
Lightning Source LLC
Chambersburg PA
CBHW040423100526
44589CB00022B/2813